The Power of a Healing Heart

Carla Deschamps

Faith and hope is the essence of purity,
which leads to having tranquility, harmony, and inner peace within you.

I started writing this book on January 4, 2022. Writing was a lifelong hobby of mine, and my safe place throughout my healing journey. Writing my thoughts and feelings during this time was my remedy and a reminder of all the love and support I've always had.

I dedicate this book in the memory of my grandparents, Ana and Rolando Alvarez. Since I was a little girl, my grandparents showed me the meaning of true, unconditional love. They were my inspiration to always follow my dreams no matter what challenges life had for me. They encouraged me to be a fighter, a conqueror, and a warrior, which is still a part of me today. My grandparents instilled in me the meaning of a healing heart and how far you can go once you are fully healed.

Thank you to ALL my loved ones and friends for your continued support!

A special thank you to my immediate family for always being by my side no matter what. I love you all unconditionally.

Table of Contents

Introduction

On February 20, 2020, an event occurred that changed my life forever: at the age of thirty-four, I was diagnosed with colon cancer. In this book, I write about my experiences and how I overcame this life-challenging event. But before I tell you my story, I want to share with you a little bit of who I am and why I decided to write this book.

My name is Carla Deschamps. I was born in the Dominican Republic; I came to the United States at the age of seven. I have two brothers and two sisters, making me the middle child. Ever since I was little, my parents taught my siblings and I to always protect and love each other no matter what. My father always said:

"You are five bodies, but united as one heart."

This phrase has been instilled in my heart ever since. I am very fortunate and blessed to have my family by my side. My family means the world to me. I am grateful for our unity and unconditional love and the support we have for one another.

I always knew that helping people was my calling and purpose. I did not know when or how, but deep in my heart, I knew that I was meant to inspire, encourage, and advocate for individuals who simply needed guidance. My parents imparted core values in me that I have carried throughout my life: love, faith, loyalty, respect, honesty, gratitude, dignity, but most importantly, empathy. Empathy has been a significant part of who I am. It has allowed me to put myself in other people's shoes, which has made a huge impact on my interactions with others.

From my life experiences, I have learned to love, value, and cherish myself more. I am extremely grateful for the woman I have become. For this reason, I wanted to write this book and share my story to inspire and encourage readers. No matter what challenges, disappointments, and mistakes we face, we as individuals can change the outcomes of our lives by the choices we make. I have been fortunate to face my challenges and overcome difficult lessons with bravery and courage. For this reason, I decided to share with you an event that I see now as a blessing because it helped me grow as a person. Hopefully, my story will also inspire you to become the highest, truest expression of yourself.

As a bonus to my book, I have included a chapter where you will be able to do self-reflections and apply some of the techniques and tools that I used during my journey. I hope that my story inspires you to create the best version of yourself by learning to understand the power of a healing heart.

Journey in the Hospital

It all started on February 17, 2020, when I, suddenly, began to feel pain on the lower right side of my stomach. The pain was indescribable. I felt a lot of tension that simply did not want to go away. My stomach was aching, and I could not bear the agony. Yet, I stayed strong because the last thing I wanted was to worry my family, especially my parents. So, for two days straight, I did not say a word to anyone about how I was feeling.

On the third day, however, I finally decided to confide in my friend, who I will call Juliette. She is someone that I care for deeply, and I know I can count on her with anything. Deep down, Juliette knew something was wrong. So, I decided to share with her what was bothering me.

Juliette took the initiative to feel my stomach and realized that it looked swollen. I was very frightened because not only was the pain consistent for three days, but my stomach now looked inflamed. All I kept thinking was "at least the swelling is not that noticeable."

But Juliette was so worried that all she kept telling me was "please, you need to go to the hospital; something doesn't feel right."

The last thing I wanted was to go to the hospital, but I knew in my heart that it was the right thing to do. After my conversation with Juliette, I contacted my brother that night and told him everything. My brother, during that time, was finishing his residency to become an emergency medicine physician. I knew that speaking with him was going to give me the last push I needed. I began to describe my physical pain and how I felt.

As a doctor, my brother recommended that I go to the emergency room the following morning. He assumed that, based on my description, my pain could be attributed to my appendix. My brother suggested that it was going to be a possibility that my appendix was going to be removed. At that moment, I felt relief because it was not as bad as I thought it would be. I decided then to go to the hospital the next day. I never would have imagined what this visit would lead to.

The following morning, I woke up very early since I had to be at the hospital by 7:00 a.m. On my way there, I tried my best to stay calm and prayed that everything was going to be alright. When I arrived at the hospital, I went directly to the emergency room just as my brother suggested. I was so nervous and kept taking deep breaths to stay at ease. Once I was checked in, the nurse technician did blood work and checked my blood pressure. He also gave me a contrast dye to drink for the imaging of my stomach and chest.

I waited for about two hours for the radiologist to call my name. All I kept thinking was "either they will find something wrong with my appendix or find kidney stones. Regardless of what they find, I hope it is not something serious. I just want this pain to go away."

I finally did my CT scan, and all I had to do was wait for my results. It was close to 10:30 a.m. when the doctor came to see me. She had this serious look on her face, and I knew something was not right. The doctor approached me and simply said, "We need to do further testing. We found something in your radiograph and before we can inform you what it is, another CT scan has to be conducted."

At that point, I did not know what to expect. I was already worried, and this news did not help. I was all alone, and I just wanted to cry. Yet, I did everything in my power to stay serene. I knew that being emotionally stressed was not going to help. All I said to the doctor was "OK."

As I waited patiently in the waiting area, I was thinking about whether I should call my brother to tell him what was happening. I did not want to worry my family. About thirty minutes passed by and a radiologist approached me once more. He conducted the CT scan and explained that within an hour or so I would receive my results.

It was close to noon when the same doctor greeted me. She looked at me and said, "I am going to get a surgeon to talk to you about your results. Give him about twenty minutes or so."

My instant thought was "oh my God, this cannot be good or get any worse." Once the doctor left, I took a deep breath and just started to cry. I couldn't take it anymore, not knowing what was wrong with me. Finally, the surgeon came and took me to a private room to speak with me.

My heart was racing! I felt extremely anxious and scared of what the doctor was going to say. I knew within me that it was going to be bad news. The doctor stared at me and with a very calming voice said, "Carla, I am so sorry for what I am going to tell you, but we wanted to make sure what it was before we told you. That is the reason why you had to take a second CT scan in order to confirm what we found in the first one. We found a mass in your colon and it is cancerous. You have colon cancer. You have to stay in the hospital because we have to do an emergency surgery to get the mass out. It is already scheduled for this Monday. Before we can conduct your surgery, on Saturday, you will need to do a colonoscopy. This will give us a better understanding of your condition."

I couldn't comprehend what the doctor was telling me. I was in complete shock and didn't even know how to respond or what to say. When I heard the word cancer, my instant thought was "is this really happening? Did I just hear that I have cancer?"

My body started to shiver, and I was so scared. I was all alone, and I only wanted someone to hug me. The doctor was trying his best to help me stay at ease, but without realizing it, I began to shed tears. At that moment, I only wanted to speak with my brother. I told the doctor to please reach out to him. I calmed myself down and stopped crying.

About five minutes later, one of the nurses called my name and informed me that my brother was on the line. As soon as I heard my brother, I immediately began to cry inconsolably.

He kept asking, "What's wrong? Why are you crying?"

With my sobbing eyes and my heart beating extremely fast, I found the courage to tell my brother that I had cancer. My brother stayed quiet for a moment.

A few seconds later, all I heard was "everything is going to be okay. Try to stay calm. You are not alone."

Hearing my brother gave me the tranquility I needed at that moment. I asked my brother not to say anything to my parents. I was not ready to tell them the news. I was in complete shock and to a certain extent still in denial. I did not want to accept the fact that I had cancer, and to make matters worse, I was not sure if it had spread to other parts of my body. So many thoughts were racing through my mind. All I kept thinking was: "How bad is this cancer? How did I even get it? How long have I had this cancer in my body? When did this happen? Why me?"

I was so overwhelmed by my own emotions and thoughts that I did not know how to react or respond to this situation. All I knew was that I needed to stay calm to process everything that was happening. Within the next few hours, I notified my mother and younger sister about what was happening. I did not want to inform my father and older siblings yet because I was still trying to grasp the news that the doctor had shared with me, but eventually, my whole immediate family knew.

On February 22, 2020, I conducted my colonoscopy in the morning. During this time, I was on a very strict liquid diet, and I could not eat anything solid. I remembered being cranky at times because I really love to eat. The nurse came to get me, and I was so frightened. I didn't even know what to expect from the procedure. Once I arrived at the surgery room, I had my doctor and a few nurses by my side. They kept telling me that everything was going to be just fine. They were very empathetic, which made me feel so much better. I closed my eyes and before I knew it, the colonoscopy was over. It only lasted about thirty minutes.

It was not as scary as I thought it would be. At this point, I was feeling optimistic because the doctor kept encouraging me throughout the process.

"The good news is that we detected the cancerous mass on time," he would say.

On that day, I made up my mind to stay positive. I was determined to do everything in my power to heal my heart from all the pain and suffering I was feeling.

"My attitude is what will make the difference," I would tell myself. At that moment, I realized how blessed and grateful I was to be alive, that faith and hope would keep me going.

The next two days, the doctor, along with the hospital staff, prepared me for my surgery, which took place on February 24, 2020. I have had surgeries in the past, but this one was, without a doubt, the most significant one yet. The day of the surgery arrived, and I was so nervous, yet calm at the same time. I knew that I was not alone because my family was cheering me on. I was as ready as I could be.

One of the nurses took me to the operating room. The doctor got there a few minutes later with a smile on his face. I knew I was in great hands. He approached me and asked, "Are you ready?"

I instantly said, "YES!" I remembered looking around the operating room wondering about what was going to happen after the surgery was over. So many thoughts were running through my mind. Yet, deep down I knew that this life lesson was going to make me stronger mentally and physically.

I looked around the operating room one last time, closed my eyes, and said a prayer asking God to protect me during the surgery. I silently prayed:

Dear Heavenly Father,

I ask today that You protect me during my surgery. You know that I have had a few surgeries in my past, but this one will be my most important one yet. I am not sure if this mass has already spread through other parts of my body, yet I am asking You to please protect me from any harm coming my way. I know that You will be with me during this journey and I will not be alone. Thank You for always taking care of me. I know I am in Your hands and nothing will go wrong. Bless me always.

In Jesus Name, Amen.

I took my last deep breath and allowed the doctor to do his magic. The surgery took about five hours. I could only imagine how my family felt waiting for the surgery to be over. I remembered waking up in my room, waiting to see my doctor. I was in a lot of pain and noticed that I had a few bandages on my stomach. I was anxious to see the doctor because I wanted to know how my surgery went. He finally arrived and said that my surgery was a total success! I have never felt so much joy and gratitude all at once. My instant thought was "I already went through the worst; my recovery will be a walk in the park."

A Moment of Gratitude

Writing in my journal and expressing gratitude has given me a feeling of inner happiness that I want you all to have. Gratitude is one of the easiest techniques to utilize to create a healthy, positive mindset. It is crucial to focus on all the blessings you already have because by doing so, you will attract more things to be grateful for. Here is an example of how I express my daily gratitude:

Thank you for my:
Eyes to see
Ears to listen
Mouth to taste
Nose to smell
Hands to feel
Feet to walk, run, and move
Heart that keeps pumping and is keeping me alive
Cells that protect my body's defenses
Immune system that keeps me strong and healthy
Blood that transport oxygen and nutrients to my lungs
Digestive system that helps my body absorb energy and growth
Brain that allows me to learn, remember, and reason as I have strong, cognitive abilities
But most importantly, I am extremely grateful for my perfect health because it allows me to enjoy life to the fullest.

2

Journey in my Recovery

I knew that recovering from the surgery was not going to be easy. Yet, I kept an optimistic attitude. Throughout the process of getting better, I told myself every day, "I am a champion. I got this. I am strong, a warrior, a fighter. It runs in the DESCHAMPS family." My demeanor and way of thinking was going to be essential for my successful recuperation.

After my surgery, my doctor came to check up on me. He was so happy with the results of the surgery and provided me with instructions on what I needed to do for the next few days. The first thing he wanted me to do was to walk for at least fifteen minutes every few hours. I did not want to move because I was in so much pain. However, I knew that walking was my first step towards my recovery.

When one of the nurses came, she asked if I was ready to go for my walk. I told her that I was and got myself ready. The nurse helped me stand up and held my hand. We began to walk slowly. As I walked, I felt discomfort but made an effort to keep going. After fifteen minutes had passed, I informed the nurse that I wanted to walk a little more. My goal was to do thirty minutes every two or three hours. The nurse asked me if I was sure, because the doctor only recommended fifteen minutes, but I wanted to push myself to do more of what was required of me. That is exactly what I did for the next few days.

I also had to do breathing exercises to expand my lungs. The nurse had given me an incentive spirometer to breathe more deeply and fully. I did the exercises on a consistent basis because my priority was to keep my lungs active and prevent any complications. I was extremely proud of myself for having such a speedy recovery. The nurses and the doctor were so impressed with how well I was doing. For the next few days, I did everything the doctor recommended with the purpose of getting discharged from the hospital.

On February 27, 2020, the doctor gave me the best news: I was finally going to be discharged. He mentioned that everything was going so well and that I could finish the rest of my recuperation in the comfort of my home. To continue walking, doing my breathing exercises, and following a strict diet, was all the doctor wanted. It was close to 5:00 p.m. when I got discharged. My parents helped me get ready. I was so happy and relieved to leave the hospital; all I desired was to see my siblings and nieces who had supported me since day one.

Once I arrived home, I spent time with my family. We were talking and laughing the whole time. I felt so much love and joy in my heart, which was exactly what I needed to tackle the next part of my recovery. Within an hour or so, I decided to rest in bed because I was physically exhausted.

The next day, my aunt and closest relatives came to visit me. It was close to noon when suddenly, I began to feel sick. I was feeling very nauseated, but I did not want to vomit. My body was still aching from the surgery, and my scars were still fresh and were healing. I was in a lot of pain. Regardless of what I wanted, my body instantly reacted, and I began to vomit. I was retching with so much force that the pain I felt was indescribable. Even worse, I vomited every five to ten minutes nonstop. I did everything I could to stop myself from vomiting, but I couldn't help it. This was occurring all day.

My parents were so worried and wanted to take me back to the hospital, but I begged them not to. However, around 7:30 p.m., I was in so much pain from vomiting that I finally told my parents to take me back. Once I arrived in the emergency room, I couldn't even speak because I was so weak. The nurse took me to a private room and gave me medication to help me with my nausea.

About an hour later, the radiologist came and did an x-ray to see what was going on with my body. In the meantime, the nurse contacted my doctor. By the time my doctor arrived, the results were in from the x-ray. My doctor came and shared with me that unfortunately I was badly constipated.

Two additional doctors arrived and told me that they were going to put a tube through my nose to help flush out my bowels. When one of the doctors began to put the tube inside my nose, she instructed me to swallow, which would allow the tube to go inside properly. Once the tube was inside, another x-ray was conducted to make sure it was where it needed to be. Having the tube inside me was the most uncomfortable feeling I could have ever imagined!

To make matters worse, my doctor informed me that I had to stay a few more days in the hospital to make sure everything was fine. He also mentioned that I was going to have the tube in my nose for at least twenty-four hours to get rid of the constipation. I was relieved that I had stopped vomiting. The nurse took me to my room where I finally had the opportunity to rest.

It took about thirty-two hours to flush my body. Just imagine having that tube in your nose for so long with no food or drink in your system. On top of that, I was so hot that I kept telling my mom, who stayed with me the whole time, to put cold water on my forehead with a cloth to ease up how I felt. At one point, I even asked one of the nurses to put the air conditioner higher for me. I had never felt so hot before and I did not know what else to do.

The doctor eventually came and took the tube out. Let me tell you, it was the best feeling ever! The next few days were tolerable. I was eating a strict liquid diet as well as going for my daily walks. On March 5, 2020, I was discharged from the hospital. Now, the next journey to my life would be my treatment, a.k.a., chemotherapy. I was praying and hoping for the best with no more surprises. This is when I closed my eyes and said my prayer:

Dear God,

I am extremely grateful that my surgery went so well, that the mass I had inside of me was completely gone. I know that these past two weeks haven't been easy, but You gave me the inner strength to bear all the pain I went through. You helped me become stronger and honestly, I did not know how strong I was until this moment. So, I ask You to please continue to give me the strength and grace in my journey of treatment because I am super scared to go through chemotherapy. But, I know that having you beside me and the love and support of my family is all that I need. Thank You for being there, especially when I need you the most. I am thankful that my faith in You has grown on a much deeper level. I love You always.

In Jesus Name, Amen.

A Moment of Gratitude

Another part of my life that to this day is important to me is LOVE. Here is one of my favorite pieces that I wrote about love:

Thank you God for blessing me with such wonderful relationships in my life. I am happy and thankful now that I have unconditional, selfless love. Love that is filled with so much vitality. Love that is pure, sincere, and genuine. My heart is full of vibrant light, peace, and harmony. I am forever grateful to have amazing, caring, valuable, strong, and exceptional people that demonstrate how much they truly care for me. Thank you, Universe, for bringing and giving me so much love.

Forever Blessed!!!

3

Journey in my Triumph

Chemotherapy! Never in a million years would I have ever thought that it would be a part of my life experience. I knew that it was going to be a challenging road ahead of me, but that was not going to stop me. More than ever, I had to set an example to my family that I was going to do everything in my power to be and to stay cancer free.

That word alone was very terrifying. All I could think of was hair loss, fatigue, nausea, vomiting, appetite changes, constipation, and other side effects. I wasn't sure whether I wanted to have treatment. The simple thought of how my body would react and how it was going to impact my family petrified me. Yet, I had a big decision ahead of me and I only had a few weeks to decide. During that time, my brother decided to have a family reunion to discuss what was best for me. I must admit I initially did not want to do chemotherapy, but after a long conversation with my family, I finally decided to go on treatment.

In the middle of March 2020, I met with my oncologist. When I first met her, I was very frightened, nervous, and anxious. She was going to go over my results from the surgery as well as inform me about my treatment moving forward. My oncologist started off by telling me that the cancer was detected right on time. I was already on Stage Two when I was diagnosed.

The oncologist expressed how lucky I was because the cancer did not spread through other parts of my body. The main reason that the cancerous mass was detected on time was because I was super skinny, which was the main reason why I even felt stomach pain. If I were thicker, I would have not felt any pain until it was too late. I was very blessed and grateful to hear the news.

Additionally, the oncologist provided me with two different treatment plans that I had to choose from. Option one was a combination of oral and injection medication that would last only three months. Option two, however, was a six-month duration, but only taking oral medication. I was still indecisive, and I did not know what to do. I had to make my decision by the last week of March, which was a period of about twelve days.

After speaking with my family and thinking about it for a few days, I finally decided to go with option one. I was going to do everything in my power to make sure to stay cancer free. Even though I was scared out of my mind, I made a commitment to myself that my health was my number one priority no matter what happened during chemo. My mindset was to stay strong and optimistic throughout this journey.

I told my oncologist that I wanted to do the three-month treatment (oral and intravenous chemotherapy) and see how my body reacted. If it was too much for my body to handle, I was going to strictly stay with oral medication even though it was a longer time span. My treatment was going to consist of taking medications for two weeks straight and one week off, as well as doing blood work and check-ins every three weeks.

On April 3, 2020, I turned thirty-five years old. It was my first day of chemotherapy. I had so much emotion that day. Even though it was my birthday, I couldn't help but feel sad and anxious because I did not know what to expect. I remembered how my nieces and sister tried their best to make me feel special. My sister brought a cake, and my family sang happy birthday. Towards the end of the night, I felt happy and filled with gratitude.

During that time, I was working from home due to the start of the Covid-19 pandemic. In a way, it was a blessing in disguise since I had already started my treatment. Working from home made me feel more at ease because I did not know what to expect regarding my physical symptoms. Within those two weeks, I was taking oral pills with a combination of IV. I noticed that it was too much for my body to handle, especially because I was very slim. I was constantly tired, felt nauseated all the time, and I barely had any appetite. For this reason, at the end of the first cycle, I informed my doctor that moving forward, I wanted to stay with oral medication only.

When I began the second cycle of my treatment, I noticed that my body reacted much better since it was only one dose versus two. I started to eat more, and my energy increased tremendously. I was feeling like my old self again, which brought me a sense of peace and happiness.

For the next few months, I took my pills on time and visited my oncologist for continued supervision. Everything was going well, and the doctor was extremely happy with the results of the treatment. To my surprise, everything that I feared did not happen. I did not lose my hair. On the contrary, it grew longer and stronger. I never had nausea the whole time I took my medication. I did not lose my appetite. Actually, the medication caused me to eat more, which helped me gain weight. The only physical symptom that I experienced was that the bottom of my feet turned black. Over time, however, it faded away. I was extremely excited when I finally finished my last cycle of chemo in October 2020.

Indeed, it was a huge accomplishment finishing my treatment the way I did. Nobody would have ever guessed that I went through this experience because of the way that I carried myself. I would tell myself that faith and hope are the essence of purity, which leads to having tranquility, harmony, and inner peace. Now more than ever, I see the importance of having these qualities to face any challenge life has in store for you.

I realized that the power of a healing heart played a significant role in my success. Throughout this journey, I did a lot of self-healing, which included my spiritual journey: praying and interacting with God. One of my prayers during this time was as followed:

Dear Heavenly Father,

Thank you for my success towards my treatment. Even though I was frightened going through chemotherapy, You showed me that anything I put my mind to is the way to be. I have learned so much throughout the past few months. I have learned to love myself more and my health became my priority. I want to take this opportunity to say, "Thank You!!" You have protected and blessed me throughout this journey. I am beyond grateful that I have blossomed into the woman I am today. Every day that passes by, I am becoming the best version of ME. And for that, I am full of love and gratitude. Always remember how much I love and respect You.

In Jesus Name, Amen.

A Moment of Gratitude

The following writing pieces express my gratitude towards life:

> *Thank you for my perfect Health. It allows me to live my life to the fullest.*
>
> *I am so happy and grateful now that I am healed. I am Cancer Free.*
>
> *I am so happy and thankful now that I have my perfect home. I get to enjoy and create memories with my family.*
>
> *I am so excited now that my wealth is increasing every day. I am traveling more frequently to my favorite places such as Paris.*
>
> *I am so happy and grateful for meeting my soulmate. We love and respect each other unconditionally.*
>
> *I am grateful for my soulmate. He helps me grow spiritually, emotionally, and mentally, but most of all he brings me peace, harmony, and endless happiness.*

4

My Healing Heart

What is my secret to a healing heart? Well, let's start from the beginning. When I first heard, "It looks like you have a cancerous mass and we need to do a colonoscopy to confirm it," I felt such a pain in my heart that words couldn't describe it. My first thought was "did I just hear that I have cancer?" My heart was racing so fast, and I had a million thoughts running through my mind. At one point, I took a deep breath and demanded my body to calm down. From that moment on, I knew that I had to decide how I was going to move forward knowing all the challenges coming my way.

When people hear the word "cancer," it is frightening, especially if you are living with the illness. Yet, as human beings, we have the power to make the choices that will make differences in our lives. I chose to be a fighter, a warrior, and a survivor, because I knew that this was NOT the end of my story. For this reason, I began my journey to heal myself and overcome all the obstacles I was going to face. You have heard of the saying, "What doesn't kill you makes you stronger." Well, now more than ever, I live by that principle.

You are probably wondering how I healed myself without going to therapy or speaking with a psychologist. The first step I took in my self-healing recovery was changing my way of thinking and attitude. I told myself: "No matter what happens, I will do everything in my power to be cancer free." With that mindset, I started to train my way of thinking by applying affirmations, meditation, motivational videos, journaling, visualization, and the significance of self-love and gratitude in my daily life. I also began to read books that empowered me to improve my self-development.

One of the techniques that has played an important role in my life is affirmations. According to Merriam-Webster, affirmation is "the act of affirming." In other words, claiming or making a declaration. When I was diagnosed with colon cancer, I began to apply affirmations which focused on health. I would tell myself on a consistent basis:

I am healthy and whole.
I have perfect health.
I am cancer free.
I am healed.

By repeating these affirmations out loud, I trained my way of thinking. I started to focus more on positive thoughts versus negative ones.

One of my favorite YouTube channels that I still listen to today is Bob Baker's. Bob Baker is known for positive self-talk and speaking about how applying affirmations can have a positive impact in your life. I listen to Bob every day, and he has been a part of my morning routine for the past three years. I am very grateful for his channel. Through him, I have learned to focus on the things I want, along with strengthening my mindset.

Other techniques that I have applied in my recovery consist of meditation and visualization. Meditation is when you quiet the mind and are fully present with your thoughts. It is about being more aware, as well as getting a better perspective of the things around you. At the beginning, meditation was difficult for me because it was hard to control my thoughts, especially when I was constantly thinking and getting distracted. However, with time, I learned to master meditation, and it has helped me tremendously. It has given me a sense of inner peace by providing a state of relaxation and tranquility of the mind.

Visualization is when you have clear mental images of something in your mind. One of the ways that I utilized visualization for my recovery was closing my eyes and visualizing myself completing chemotherapy with success. I imagined my body strong and healthy, my hair not falling out, and exercising to keep my body in shape.

I did this technique as often as I could during the day on a continuous basis.

Visualization is a powerful tool to use because the brain doesn't know what is real and what isn't. For this reason, visualizing myself as healthy was an excellent way to tell my body that I was perfectly fine. Until this day, this technique remains as a part of my daily life.

Additional YouTube motivational videos have played a significant impact in my recovery, including TD Jakes, Joel Osteen, and Tony Robbins. My sister recommended Les Brown, who is also an amazing motivational speaker. Listening to Les helped me to become the best version of myself. I started to realize that loving and investing in myself more was the best thing I could have done to become the person I wanted to be.

One of the ways to become the best version of myself was to set short-term goals that I wanted to achieve, including weight gain. During that time, I weighed 103 lbs., the skinniest I have ever been. My goal was to gain weight and be at least 115 lbs. That required changing my diet completely to reach my goal. So, for the next few months, I began to eat more, drink protein shakes, along with incorporating exercise at least three to four times a week.

By August 2020, I had reached my goal of weighing 116 lbs. and my physical body was at its best. I loved seeing myself in the mirror knowing how astonishing I looked. My family couldn't believe how gaining weight and exercising daily changed my physical appearance for the better. Everyone around me kept telling me that I had a special glow within me. This felt amazing and brought me to the realization that self-improvement can impact my life in a positive way.

Journaling has also been a favorite technique I used during my recovery. Since I can remember, journaling has been a part of me. It has allowed me to express my thoughts and feelings in a productive manner. Both Rhonda Byrne, who wrote The Secret, and Andrew Kap, who wrote The Last Law of Attraction Book You'll Ever Need to Read: The Missing Key to Finally Tapping Into the Universe And Manifesting Your Desires, played important roles in how I journaled. Both books focused on how to manifest what you truly want in life. During my recovery, my focal point was my health.

A technique that Kap shared in his book was called, The Story Scripting Method. This method consists of journaling as if you are already living what you truly desire. He encourages writing things into existence (in the present tense form) and feeling what it would be like if what you wanted were already here. On April 18, 2020, I wrote my first story scripting method:

I am so thankful to be in such wonderful health. My cells are duplicating in vibrant, healing ways in order to protect and support my body. My immune system is getting stronger everyday as I eat healthy foods such as fruits and vegetables. I am full of light, positive energy that allows me to see, hear, touch, taste, and feel everything around me. Thank you, Universe, for giving me perfect health. This gives me the opportunity to do all of the things that bring me so much joy. I love the fact that my body reacts in such luminous, radiant ways when I take my medication. I am so happy and grateful for my health because I get to engage with all the people I love and adore. I have the power to control my health, which is bright, full of energy and vitality. I am blessed to have a strong heart, lungs, and an extraordinary digestive system. I can exercise every day as well as meditate in order to keep building a powerful, potent, vigorous mindset. Thank You, God, for allowing me to keep going every day. I am grateful for my eyes, nose, ears, mouth, hands, feet, heart, immune system, veins, lungs, cells, and ALL of my body parts for helping me have my perfect health. Thank you, Universe, for bringing into my life the most radiant, vibrant, positive healing energy a girl can ask for. I am blessed to have an abundance of health. Thank you for my healing scars and making me Cancer Free!! I am grateful for my second chance in life.

This scripting was the essence of the power of self-love and gratitude. Without these two qualities, my recovery would not have been the same. I am extremely grateful for all the life lessons I have learned in the past three years. I have grown so much mentally, physically, and spiritually. I love the woman that I have become. Despite everything, I am blessed to be alive.

Looking back, being diagnosed with colon cancer has been a blessing in disguise. I appreciate life more and am open to new and endless opportunities. I will be forever grateful for this experience making me the woman I am today. I hope that my story inspires and encourages you so that you know that no matter what challenges or obstacles you face, learning to heal your heart and spirit will give you a sense of inner peace and happiness.

Always remember how extraordinary and beautiful you are. You are strong, abundant, loved, blessed, kind, healthy, fortunate, worthy, successful, confidant, noble, honorable, and brilliant. Be ready and open to receive what life has in store for you. You deserve nothing but the best. I want to end my memoir by sharing this prayer with you:

Dear God,

I want to take this opportunity to tell You how much I love and respect You. Thank You for giving me the strength to overcome my fears, challenges, and obstacles. Thank You for Your devoted love. I am grateful and happy to call You my Father in heaven. Today, I pray for my continued strength, wisdom, and inner peace. Let there be light. Let there be unconditional selfless love. Let there be harmony, hope, and faith in my heart. Please protect me from any harm or negative auras that's around me. From this moment on, I draw and receive vitality, prosperity, love, victory, health, and joy into my life. Thank You for ALL of my blessings.

In Jesus Name, Amen.

A Moment of Gratitude

Other gratitude scripts that helped me throughout my journey include the following:

Thank you for my healing scars. It is a symbol of overcoming hardships as well as being a true conqueror. My scars signify inner strength and courage.

I am so thankful now that I am well. It allows me to do all the things I love such as exploring new places and interacting with my friends and family. Knowing that I am well gives me the power to stand tall no matter what life has in store for me.

I am grateful for my beating heart. It represents that I am alive and well. Definitely something worth smiling about.

I am so happy and grateful now that I have radiant, positive energy. It gives me an inner glow that is contagious as others love to be around me. It is as bright as the sun, making everything shine.

I am grateful for the unconditional love of those around me. Thank you for self-love.

I am grateful for my strength, power, independence, protection, stamina, stability, wisdom, transformation, bravery, solitude, generosity, unconditional love, self-confidence, courage, self-worth, patience, and an awakening of the mind. I hold the power to dictate my story. I have the power to control my destiny.

5

My Most Sacred Moments

As you have read, my journey of being diagnosed with colon cancer at such a young age was a breakthrough in my life. I learned that utilizing the power of your mind can change everything: meditation, affirmations, journaling, prayer, and visualization all aided my recovery. I consider these techniques my most sacred moments.

However, the most sacred writing pieces that were crucial to me was when I wrote down my mantras, which focused on my life experiences as well as my self-worth as a woman. My mantras consisted of the following:

> *My life experiences have given me the opportunity for personal growth and development. It has provided me with the feelings of pride, self-worth, self-love, and the essence of accepting and loving myself each and every day.*

> *From this moment on, I release any negative thinking, anxiety, or fear and allow myself to be a confident, optimistic, and assertive person in order to grow spiritually, physically, emotionally, and mentally.*

> *I believe in myself, and I am proud of the woman I have become. I attract more self-love, self-confidence, and self-worth into my life. Today, I walk with confidence and a sense of inner peace and happiness.*

*From this moment on, I will love myself more. I will attract
more happiness and success into my life. I am worthy of love. I
am strong, brave, hard working, self determined, warrior,
survivor, fighter, beautiful, powerful, loving, and
compassionate. I am full of light with a positive, radiant
energy.*

As you can see, journaling has played a significant role throughout my healing journey. It has helped me focus on all the things I wanted in my life as well as becoming the woman I choose to become. In the next chapter, you will have the opportunity to self-reflect on your own personal journeys and apply these techniques as a starting point towards healing.

6

Your Journey Towards Self Healing

The first step towards self-healing is to identify what area or areas in your life you are genuinely struggling with. It is extremely important that you are completely honest with yourself. Remember, this is your journey, and it all starts with being truthful and honest. These are two qualities you will need to healing your heart. I know that looking inside yourself can be challenging and at times scary, but it is a necessary step to self-healing.

In this chapter, I will guide you through this process by giving you the tools and techniques that I utilized, so that you can apply them in your daily lives. Let's start with affirmations.

Part One - Identify Your Inner Struggles / Affirmations

I want you to go to a place which brings you inner peace. A place where you are most comfortable. A place with no distractions. It could be somewhere in your household or outside. Once you choose your place, I would like you to close your eyes for a moment and listen to your own beating heart. Be mindful and pay attention. Once you identify a specific area you want to improve in, whether it is health, wealth, love, confidence, or so forth, I want you to come up with your own affirmations. Starting affirmations can be as follows:

I am _____

I have _____

I can _____

I will _____

Example:

In my personal journey, I focused heavily on health. For this reason, my personal affirmations consisted of the following:

> **I am** healthy, whole, and full of vitality. It has given me the opportunity to create new memories with the people I love. Waking up every morning gives me a sense of purpose. I know that my journey in this world is just beginning.

> **I have** a healthy mind, body, and soul. It provides me with a clear vision of who I want to be along with where I want to go. Everything I need is already within me.

I can heal my body with daily exercises and taking deep breaths. It allows me to have a strong, healthy physique, which is my temple. My mood and energy instantly improve.

I will nurture my body with good food, sleep, and self-care. It gives me the stamina to keep moving forward and face challenges with bravery and resistance. Taking care of myself is my number one priority.

Once you create your own affirmations, repeat them either out loud or silently at least three to five times a day, preferably in the morning and at night. Reprogramming your mindset is extremely essential to making the proper changes in the areas you would like to build on. The more you repeat and feel your affirmations, the more effective they will be.

I also recommend listening to affirmations a few minutes a day. Some of my favorite YouTube channels include Bob Baker, Be Inspired, and Unlimited You. Listening to affirmations daily not only makes you feel amazing, but also allows you to be proactive with your daily routines. This will help you build better, healthier habits that will benefit you in the long run.

Part Two - Meditation / Visualization

Other effective techniques include meditation and visualization. These methods will allow you to unclutter your thoughts. Meditation is best practiced when you are in sync with your body and mind. It gives you the opportunity to focus on the present as well as increase self-awareness. By meditating, not only will you decrease your stress level, but you will gain a new perspective about the areas in your life you want to change.

Meditation takes practice and patience. There are different ways to meditate. In the beginning, I listened to guided meditations to keep me focused. One of the YouTube channels I used the most was Great Meditation. I also utilized an app called Headspace. Other ways consist of mindfulness, walking, and body scanning. Do not get discouraged if you feel that while you are meditating, your thoughts tend to wonder. That is completely normal. The best way to keep your focus is by concentrating on your breath. Regardless of which technique you decide to do, meditation is an excellent tool to practice to quiet down the mind.

Moreover, visualization is another method you can try with the purpose of increasing your emotional and physical wellness. As I have shared with you, visualization is when you have a clear, specific image in your mind of what you want to achieve. In my case, I visualized myself being cancer free and having perfect health. In my mind, I would picture myself exercising, eating healthy foods, and drinking plenty of water to keep my body hydrated.

I want you to visualize yourself doing things you want as well as achieving the goals you want to accomplish. This will allow your mind to know specifically what your heart truly desires. Visualization can be done within a few seconds or minutes. It is totally up to you. Other ways you can visualize are by creating a vision board, listening to guided visualization meditation, and having a written vision statement. The more you practice this technique, the more real it will feel, which eventually will turn into your reality.

Part Three -Journaling

Journaling is the best tool to utilize to heal from any wounds you might be feeling. It is an excellent way to express yourself in a positive, productive way. Throughout my journey, not only did I express my feelings and worries in writing, but it allowed me to process my experiences in an effective manner. It helped me focus on my recovery along with identifying all my goals. In my journal, I wrote my affirmations, stated my daily gratitude, and noted my story scripting in areas of my life that I wanted to change. I used journaling to retrain my way of thinking and created a positive, healthy mindset.

I would love for you to do the same. Give yourself the opportunity to write down your feelings and worries in a journal. One of the advantages is that journaling helps the brain stay focused, which ultimately boosts your memory and gain self-confidence. I know that not everyone is comfortable expressing themselves in a journal, but it is worth trying. Based on my personal experiences, journaling is not only a great asset to help you address your concerns, but it will also improve your overall mood. Remember, there is no right or wrong way to practice this technique. When you write from the heart, everything will fall into place.

7

A Final Note to You

Even though I do not know who you are, I will forever be in spirit, wishing you a life full of peace, light, serenity, and tranquility. Always remember how extraordinary and blessed you are. No matter what happens, you have the power to change anything in your life. May today and always bring you lots of love, success, wealth, health, and happiness. Now, read this prayer with me as I read it with you:

Dear Heavenly Father,

Today, I ask that You enter my life as I need Your unconditional love, guidance, and support. May Your faith, grace, wisdom, and sincerity lead my way to fulfill my truest, highest expression of myself. Thank You for giving me the opportunity to learn from my past to live my present with the purpose to have a bright, successful future. I know that having You by my side will give me the power to keep moving forward even when life challenges me throughout the way. My faith in You will be the fuel to always do what is right even when others hurt or disappoint me. Help me become the person that I am meant to be to also inspire, encourage, and be of service to others as You have shown us. I am forever grateful for my inner strength, inner peace, and wholehearted selfless love. I love You today and always.

In Jesus Name, Amen.

 **To My Readers**

I am happy and genuinely thankful for you taking your time to read my book. I hope that moving forward, your life turns out exactly how you envisioned it. I know that at times, life can be challenging, but remember that you are stronger than you think. I believe in you!

 ## Acknowledgments

I want to take this moment and give a special thank you to my family for their unconditional support. You have helped me overcome so many challenges throughout my life, especially with my health. I am beyond grateful for having such an amazing, loving, and caring family. You have helped me become a stronger version of myself.

In addition, I want to say thank you to the following people who were significant in their contribution to my book. They are:

Christina De Lucia, my best friend, who has been with me since day one. Thank you for always taking the time to provide your feedback and helping to make this book more meaningful.

Heather Zahn, for taking the time to revise and edit my book. Thank you for all of the suggestions you provided me.

Jennifer Dmytrow, for doing the illustrations for my book. Without you even knowing, your art represented three important people in my life that are now in heaven. Thank you for the dedication you put into my book.

Amanda Rosa and Qualia C. Hendrickson, for your continued support and guidance. You helped me in this amazing journey. Thank you for helping me turn this book into reality.

My sister, Carla Deschamps, who has been my rock. And yes, we have the same name and no, we are not twins. I am grateful for the endless hours of reading and the pointers you gave me to make my book more personal. Thank you for all the times you have encouraged me to become the woman I am today. I am thankful to you for introducing me to motivational videos and the importance of implementing affirmations into my daily life.

Jose Deschamps, my baby brother. Without realizing it, you saved my life and gave me the extra push I needed to go to the hospital. Because of your perseverance, I was able to treat my cancer on time, giving me a second chance. You are conscientious, extraordinary, talented, brilliant, and an inspiration to all of us, so thank you for being you. But yet again, that is what doctors do. I am beyond proud.

THANK YOU ALL!!!

Words cannot express my love, respect, and gratitude.

Carla Deschamps was born in the Dominican Republic and came to the United States at the age of seven. Currently working with elementary-school level children, Carla has always known that helping others was her calling. Her aspiration is for her students to become the best versions of themselves. After being diagnosed with cancer at the age of thirty-four, Carla learned the power of her mind, and how her thoughts could help her heal. Carla is the middle child of her family, with two brothers and two sisters, and comes from a loving family, all of whom supported her through her traumatic journey. She has a passion for life and believes that it is significant to always live in the present moment.

Carla has a strong belief in the power of positive thinking, and she has learned how to conquer negative thoughts living by this principle. The Power of a Healing Heart is Carla's first book.

Printed in Great Britain
by Amazon

29819478R00024